THE STORY OF NOAH

A JOURNEY OF FAITH, HOPE & NEW BEGINNINGS

CHRISTIAN LOWE

Copyright © 2025

All rights reserved. No part of this book may be reproduced in any form without written permission from the publisher.

This book is a work of fiction. Names, characters, places, and incidents are either products of the author's imagination or used fictitiously. Any resemblance to actual events or locales or persons, living or dead, is entirely coincidental.

The publisher and author have made every effort to ensure the accuracy of the information herein. However, the information contained in this book is sold without warranty, either express or implied. Neither the author nor the publisher shall be liable for any damages arising here from.

Introduction

In a land where the skies once sparkled with laughter and hope, something had changed. People forgot what kindness felt like—they argued too loudly, cared too little, and the world felt a little darker each day. But hidden among the whispers of worry stood a young man named Noah.

Noah loved adventure—he loved the feel of fresh wood under his fingertips, the smell of blooming flowers at dawn, and the way the stars winked above him each night. What made Noah most special wasn't his curious nature—it was his heart. His heart for God. He believed that goodness mattered. He believed in promise. And above all, he believed in trust.

Every sunset, Noah would kneel in his quiet garden beside his family—his loving wife and strong sons—and thank God for the day's wonder. In those moments, his heart felt brave. Like it could start something new.

But the world around him had grown heavy with sadness. Rivers ran too slow. Animals wandered too far from home. And people, well—they lost their way.

One evening, as fireflies danced around him and crickets sang goodnight, Noah felt something different. A gentle knowing deep inside, like someone calling his name. It stirred a firm but quiet voice in his spirit, saying—build.

Build what? Noah didn't know yet. But his heart told him it was important.

This is the beginning of a story about obedience, trust, and new beginnings. A story of a promise that breaded through dark storms and flooded lands. A story where one young man's heart became the spark of new hope for everyone.

So come along, brave reader—for you're about to sail into a journey of courage, wonder, and promise. Welcome to The Story of Noah.

Chapter 1:
A Heart for God – Choosing Obedience

Noah awoke that morning to the soft glow of lantern light dancing across the wooden beams in his home. The air smelled of fresh bread, and the sound of his mother humming drifted from the kitchen. His little brothers scurried past in their sandals, feathers tulled everywhere from the chickens they had helped feed. But despite these happy sounds and familiar routines, something in the air felt heavy—as though the world itself sighed.

Outside, the wind carried distant grumbles and raised voices. Neighbors argued over small things; laughter seemed rare and rushed. Even the birds circled overhead with wary wings. Yet in his heart, Noah felt a spark of light.

"God, help me do what's right," he whispered as he finished his morning chores.

He listened for an answer, and though the day remained quiet, Noah sensed a calm assurance slowly settle deep within him. A nudge in his soul—soft, kind, trusting.

Later, while Noah and his father worked in the shed, shaping and sanding wood, the gentle voice inside him came again.

"Build."

Noah paused, heart pounding. "Build… what, God?" he wondered in awe.

The voice didn't come in thunder or wind—it came in his heart. Simple. Clear.

"Tell your family," Noah said with a gentle firmness, handing his chisel to his father. "God has asked me to build something."

His father paused mid-stroke. Mother set down her tools. His brothers stood still, their eyes wide. Around them, the shed went quiet—fear mingling with curiosity.

"Build what?" his father asked. His voice trembled.

Noah didn't know all the answers yet. He only knew he would obey. "I don't know just yet," he admitted. "But I feel—this is God's call."

The family looked at each other. Some hearts felt unsure. Others, like Noah's, quietly whispered hope. His mother reached for Noah's hand. "Alright, Noah. We'll do this together."

But word of Noah's plans spread fast. The neighbors laughed and whispered, "Build what? A giant boat? There hasn't been rain in years!" Some shook their heads, while others sneered.

That night, as dark clouds began to gather and chatter grew cold, Noah lay in bed with his brothers tucked close. He could hear the wind outside, carrying the voices: "He's crazy." "Don't be fooled." But inside his own chest, his heart felt steady.

"Tomorrow," he thought, "we begin."

Chapter 2:
Building the Ark – Faith in Action

A week later, the morning sun stretched through the trees as Noah stepped into the forest with his sons, tools in hand. The birds chattered overhead, curious about the work that was about to begin. In the midst of that quiet morning air, the first giant oak log was felled—thud!—and the adventure truly began.

1. Gathering the Timbers

- Noah and his sons hewed, sawed, and shaped the wood together.

- Their muscles ached, but their spirits kept them going—especially when their mother brought fresh bread and honey-sweetened tea to the worksite.

- Laughter and teamwork echoed under the open sky.

2. Mysteries and Measurements

- Noah spread the mysterious plan on parchment, showing curved lines and strange angles.

- "This isn't like any house—or boat—we've ever built!" his eldest son exclaimed.

- With each measurement, the ark's shape came into view: long, wide, and built to hold something extraordinary.

3. The Mockers Appear

- The villagers gathered, arms folded. "Noah, what are you building?" they jeered.

- One neighbor called it a "fool's timber heap." Another laughed, "You'll float this on mud, Noah?"

- Yet Noah answered calmly: "We build because God told us to."

4. Working Through the Day

- As midday sun beat down, Noah zipped the hammer, the drill, and the laughter.

- Dust danced in the beams of light; sawdust covered their feet like golden snow.

5. Rain and Resolve

- Storm clouds darkened the sky—something else entirely was brewing.

- A sudden downpour drenched the worksite. The villagers cheered and scattered, but Noah and his family continued.

- They tightened wood, secured joints, and placed fresh planks. Together, they trusted—and built.

6. A Towering Creation

- By sunset, the ark rose tall against the sky—long and solid, gliding over its frame.

- Neighbors watched in astonishment, their laughter faltering.

- The shape of God's promise stood before them—proof that faith, acted upon, can create the unbelievable.

Chapter 3:
The Great Flood – God's Promise

Darkness gathered at the edges of the sky long before the rain began. Noah stood at the door of the ark with his family and the array of animals, wide-eyed at the ocean of clouds rolling overhead. The wind rose, whistling through the unsealed gaps, carrying with it a chill that spoke of changing times.

Drops of rain tapped the wooden deck—tiny at first, like a billion little fingers drumming to a secret tune. Then they came harder. Noah heard the thrum and felt the world shudder beneath him. His heart raced, but his lips whispered a prayer: "God, You are with us."

All around them, the animals stirred. A pair of doves cooed softly from their perches. A cacophony of roars, chirps, bleats, and snorts filled the air as every living creature found its place in the crowded halls of the ark. With steady hands, Noah and his sons closed the heavy door, and wood locked into place.

When the rain fell, it did so in sheets—a symphony of water pounding against the ark's sides. Everyone huddled inside: the lions nestled beside the lambs, the elephants swayed gently in unison. Fear tried to creep in, but Noah's calm presence was a reminder of hope. Wherever his eyes landed—his wife, his sons, the animals—he saw a flicker of trust.

He gathered his family in the central hold. "Hold tight," he said softly, "God promised He would keep us safe." As thunder boomed, their small hands found each other. Together, they bowed in prayer:

"Thank You for Your promise. Thank You that we are safe."

Outside, the waters lifted the ark as if it weren't wood at all but a feather on the wind. Towers of water swelled all around, and the world vanished beneath the waves.

Time passed in days and nights stitched together by the rhythm of rain. In the darkness, Noah's prayers never wavered; his faith never faltered. He reminded his family with each new dawn (and every thunderclap) that God was watching, protecting, holding them steady in the storm.

One morning, the rain slowed—just enough for a hush to settle inside. Through a tiny window high above, Noah saw it: a curtain of gray lifting, a soft glow that promised a shift. He knelt in silence, feeling the promise echo in his bones: the worst was still outside, but hope—real, living hope—was growing inside him.

Chapter 4:
Dove and Rainbow – Promise Remembered

A hush fell over the ark as the final drops of rain trickled down. Noah rose, heart pounding, and made his way to the upper deck. He opened the small window wide enough to let in the fresh, crisp air. A thin mist drifted across the flooded horizon—but then, a gentle flutter.

Noah held his breath as he released the first dove, its wings white as clouds against the gray sky. The bird soared into the mist but returned soon after, clutching a small, green olive leaf. Cheers of delight and relief echoed across the ark.

"Look!" Noah cried, lifting the leaf for all to see. His family crowded beside him, their faces alight with hope. The rain might have fallen, but proof of new life had arrived.

The dove was sent again. This time, it flew higher, circling through clearing skies. When it did not return, silence fell… until Noah's soft, brave words:

"Maybe she has found New Ground." A hopeful hush lingered in every heart.

Days passed. The ark floated in a world transformed—blanketed in water, yet moving toward something brighter. Then, one morning, a rainbow appeared. It arced across the sky in vibrant bands of red, orange, yellow, green, blue, and violet. Noah's eyes filled with wonder.

"God's bow," he whispered. "His promise."

He called for his family. They gathered on the wet deck, rain boots splashing in puddles. Above them, color shimmered. Above them, a covenant—silent but powerful.

Noah knelt and prayed. "Thank You, God, for keeping Your promise."

A calm settled over the ark. The animals, sensing the shift, moved closer together—but this time in peace, not fear. Even the rivers of water around them seemed to shimmer with the rainbow's glow.

Noah gently touched the wood beneath him. This ark—once a rescue—now held a message. A message of trust kept, of storms passed, and of new beginnings blooming just beyond.

Chapter 5:
Starting Again – New Beginnings

The ark's heavy door creaked open against the sound of gentle dripping. Noah stepped onto firm ground for the very first time in what felt like forever. Beneath his feet was soft, damp earth—no longer water. Around him, the world was quiet, waiting.

Noah lowered his sons one by one, then helped his wife follow. They stood together on fresh soil, feeling the gentle rise and fall of the land. Every drop of rain had settled into a calm silence that hummed with possibility.

Around them, timid green shoots pushed through the mud. Noah knelt and picked a tender sprout. He turned to his family, eyes bright with promise. "This is our new beginning," he said softly. "We will plant seeds, build homes, and love this world again."

The animals stepped carefully from the ark—lions and lambs, goats and giraffes—all blinking under the open sky. They sniffed the earth and looked to the waiting humans, ready to rebuild their lives alongside them. Noah watched, heart full, as the creatures formed their own little families: birds gathering twigs, rabbits hopping toward open fields.

That day, families worked as one. Noah and his sons carried stones and wood to build a small shelter. His wife and daughters began planting seeds—wheat, vegetables, flowers. Laughter returned, soft but certain. The world seemed to breathe alongside them.

As dusk settled, they gathered around a new table made from freshly hewn wood. Candles flickered, casting warm light on their faces. They held hands—humble, grateful. Noah smiled and offered a prayer of thanks:

"Thank You, God, for this land, for our family, and for Your promise that a new beginning is always possible."

Then, to celebrate, his son offered a small song—a melody about the sun rising, the seeds growing, and hope that lives in every heart. The rest joined in, soft voices floating into the starry sky.

In that moment, Noah looked up and saw the same stars that had guided him before the flood. They seemed brighter now, full of possibility. He thought of the journey—of obedience, of trust, of storms—and realized that every step, every nail, every prayer had led them here: to a world renewed.

And just like Noah, each reader—each child—can start again with hope, faith, and a heart ready to build something beautiful.

www.ingramcontent.com/pod-product-compliance
Lightning Source LLC
Chambersburg PA
CBHW082129280925
33292CB00005B/29